Adolfo Pierra

The Cuban patriots, a drama of the struggle for

independence actually going on in the gem of the Antilles

Adolfo Pierra

The Cuban patriots, a drama of the struggle for independence actually going on in the gem of the Antilles

ISBN/EAN: 9783337306427

Printed in Europe, USA, Canada, Australia, Japan

Cover: Foto ©Andreas Hilbeck / pixelio.de

More available books at **www.hansebooks.com**

The Cuban Patriots,

A DRAMA

OF THE STRUGGLE FOR INDEPENDENCE ACTUALLY
GOING ON IN THE GEM OF THE ANTILLES.

IN THREE ACTS.

WRITTEN IN ENGLISH BY

A NATIVE CUBAN.

PHILADELPHIA:

1873.

INTRODUCTION.

THIS drama was not inspired under the excitement produced by the butcheries of the ill-fated Virginius prisoners; nor is its object to add fuel to the flame of just indignation enkindled by the revolting atrocities perpetrated by the Spaniards in Cuba. The plan was conceived five or six months ago, and ever since the author has devoted to the work every minute of time he could spare from his regular occupations.

The aim of the play is to present a faithful picture of the stirring events, manners, and life in the Central Department of that unfortunate island during the first half year of the present struggle for independence. The action is laid in Puerto Principe (the author's birthplace) and surrounding country.

Although the battle in the last act did not take place as represented, it is within the bounds of likelihood. Several engagements of about the same magnitude occurred at the time in that same district (Camaguey), in one of which, at least, the Spanish troops, under General Puello, were defeated with very serious losses.

The requirements of the plot have compelled the author to locate Señor Blanco's hacienda close to the Cascorro Mountain, when in fact no hacienda of any importance is found within ten or twelve miles of it; but this does not impair the versimilitude of the action. A great many well-to-do, and even wealthy families, in that part of the island abandoned the cities at the commencement of the revolution, under the impression that they would be safer in their country properties; but hunted subsequently by the Spanish troops with fiendish eagerness, they were often forced to seek refuge in the density of the forests or the fastnesses of the mountains, this being particularly the case with those families whose male relatives were in the ranks of the patriots. No pen—no language could convey an accurate idea of the sufferings then endured by disabled old men, invalid matrons, delicate maids, and tender children.

In regard to the ferocity displayed by the Spaniards, both regulars and volunteers, in their war against the Cuban patriots, the author has purposely avoided touching the extremes. Acts of cruelty have been committed by them too revolting to be exhibited on the stage. Even in portraying the Spanish characters brought forth in the drama, the writer has endeavored to be moderate and just.

Whether the author has been able to carry out his design; whether he has succeeded in so working up the action as to make it interesting; whether his characters are well delineated and sustained, are questions for an enlightened public to decide.

THE AUTHOR.

PHILADELPHIA., PA., Dec. 8, 1873.

PRONUNCIATION AND EXPLANATION

OF SPANISH NAMES AND WORDS USED IN THIS DRAMA.

Almanegra, *al'mah-nay'grah.*

Angel Castillo, *Ahn'hel Casteel'lyoe.*

Antonio Blanco, *An-ton'nyoe Blan'coe.*

Augusto Arango, *Ahoo-goos'toe Ah-ran'goe.*

Bayamo, *Bah-ee-ah'mo.*

Caballero, *cah-bal-lyer'oh*, gentleman, sir.

Canalito, *can-al-eet'oe.*

Cascorro, *Cas-cor'roh.*

Cisneros, *Cis-ner'os.*

Cortez, *Corteth'.*

Conchita, *Con-tchee'tah.*

Cuba, *Coo'bah.*

Cubitas, *Coo-bee'tahs.*

Diego, *Deedy'goe.*

Don Juan, *Done' Hoo-an'.*

Enrique, *En ree'kay.*

Guanaja, *Goo-ah-nah'hah.*

Guaimaro, *Goo-ah'eem-ah-roe.*

Jiguani, *Hee-goo-ah-nee'.*

Linarez, *Lee-nar'eth.*

Machete, *mah-tchay'tay*, a cutlass, two to three feet long, used by Cuban peasants to clear away bushes, etc., and also as a weapon.

Mambi, *mam-beeh'*, a nickname applied by the Spaniards to the Cuban patriots.

Mendez, *Men'deth.*

Manigua, *man-eeh' goo-ah,* bushes.

Miranda, *Me-ran'dah.*

Montero, *Mon-tay'roe.*

Niño, masculine, *nin'nyo*, Niña, feminine, *nin'nyah*, child, infant. These terms are used by the slaves in Cuba before the names of all white persons except their head masters and mistresses.

Perez, *Payr'eth.*

Perico, *Pay-ree'koe*

Puerto Principe, *Poo-ayr'toe Preen'cee-pay.*

Quesada, *Kay-sah'dah.*

Ricardo, *Re-car'doe.*

Sabana, *sah-bah'nah.* A large plain, often covered with palmettoes, and sometimes dotted with palm-trees.

Señor, *sen-nyore'*, lord, sir, mister.

Señorita, *sen-nyor-ee'tah*, miss, young lady.

Tellez, *Te'lyeth.*

Yara, *Yar'ah.*

Valmaseda, *Val-mah-say'dah.*

Viva Cuba libre, *vee'vah Coo'bah lee'bray*, Long live free Cuba! hurrah for free Cuba!

Viva España, *veevah Es-pan-nyah*, Long live Spain!

DRAMATIS PERSONÆ.

Ricardo Agudo, patriot general.
Señor Antonio Blanco, a rich hacendado.
Enrique, his son, a Cuban colonel.
Colonel ⎱
General ⎰ *Almanegra*, of the Spanish army.
Colonel Ramsey, an American in the Cuban service.
Captain Montero, of the Spanish army.
Don Juan, a Spanish volunteer.
A Lieutenant, ⎰
A Sergeant, ⎱ Spanish volunteers.
A Corporal, ⎰
Perico, a negro slave.
A Cuban Aid-de-camp.
A Cuban Surgeon.
A Spanish Sergeant.

Conchita Blanco.
Rosita Blanco.
Camila, a middle-aged mulatto servant.

Spanish Volunteers, Cuban Patriots, Negro Slaves.

Time of action.—ACT. I. December, 1868; ACTS II. and III. April, 1869.

☞ For costumes and properties, see last page.

ACT I.

SCENE I.—*Elegant drawing room in Señor Antonio Blanco's house in Puerto Principe; walls painted white or a light color; large main door, one shutter open, U. R.; large window, shutters wide open, with light iron railing on street, L. R.; door in flat, C., communicating with bed-room; large arched door, without shutters, L., leading into dining-room; a piano, mahogany cane-bottomed sofa and rocking-chairs, R., between door and window; carpet between sofa and rocking-chairs; round marble table with newspapers, C.; chandelier lighted, cane-bottomed chairs, pictures, &c. Time—night.*

Enter RICARDO AGUDO *and* ENRIQUE BLANCO, R.; *take off and lay their hats on centre-table.*

Ricardo. My dear Enrique, I have highly important information to communicate to you privately.

Enrique. I am impatient to hear it; but let us first make sure that we are not heard. We have to be extremely cautious just now. (*Goes up to window, R, followed by* RICARDO).

Enr. (*pointing off*). Do you see those volunteers in that corner shop?

Ric. I do.

Enr. Our house is closely watched by them. (*They come down,* C.) Oh, Ricardo! you, that have just arrived from the United States—from that classical land of liberty—do not know all we have had to suffer here lately. It was bad enough when we had to endure the despotism of the Spanish government alone; but since we are in the power of the volunteers, it is a hundred times worse. You won't recognize our native city. Puerto Principe is deserted to-day, half her dwellings abandoned to the rapacity of the volunteers,—of those men, who come to Cuba penniless, enrich themselves, and then become our worst enemies!

Ric. How I long for the moment when I can face them in the field!

Enr. Face them in the field! They won't give us the chance. They will let the regular army do all the fighting, whilst they will hold to the cities, seaports, and fortified places, where in safety they can oppress the defenceless inhabitants, and gloat over the bloody executions of the unfortunate patriots who may fall into their merciless hands.

Ric. The villains! But we ought rather to be thankful to them, Enrique. They are learning us that we have nothing to expect from Spain in the way of justice and liberty, and they have thus assured our ultimate independence.

Enr. But to your news.

Ric. I am coming to it. When I first heard in the United States the tidings of the Revolutionary outbreak of Yara, I resolved to come right off and join my brothers in the field. Having served in the Union army, my little military experience I knew would be of some value to my beloved country; but desiring to bring some material of war, which we so sorely need, I came first to Nassau, where in company with General Quesada and other patriots, I succeeded in loading a schooner with a cargo of arms and ammunition. As I was not yet suspected by the Spaniards, I came by steamer, *via* Havana, in the ordinary way, and I have been these three days anxiously waiting to hear from that expedition. And now *(lowering his voice)* I have received private advice to the effect that General Quesada has succeeded in safely landing the arms at Guanaja.

Enr. (delighted) Hurrah! My dear boy, give me your hand *(they shake hands warmly)*. That is a Godsend to us. Why did you keep it so long from me?

Ric. I must be off to-night, join my men in the Cubitas Mountains, and proceed under Gen. Quesada to distribute the arms where they may do most good.

Enr. I would like to accompany you, Ricardo.

Ric. You only anticipate my wishes. Being well acquainted with that part of the country, you are the very man I want. Besides, by your influence among the peasants of that region, where one of your father's haciendas is, you can help to increase our forces.

Enr. I have already over a hundred good men there, who only await my orders to move; but they are poorly armed. Scarcely one-half of them have firearms, mostly shot-guns.

Ric. They will be well armed within twenty-four hours. Get ready to depart. I only wait to see Conchita—I mean your father and sisters, and bid them good-bye.

Enr. They will soon be home. I left them at uncle Diego's. You know that his family is preparing to leave the city with father and sisters. To-morrow, before daybreak they will start for our hacienda on the Cascorro Mountains.

Ric. I hope they will be safer there.

Enr. (crossing to window). I think I hear them coming. Yes, here they are.

Enter SEÑOR ANTONIO BLANCO, CONCHITA, *and* ROSITA, R.
SEÑOR ANTONIO, *crosses the stage greatly agitated, deposits his hat and walking-cane on piano, recrosses, and sits on rocking-chair, rocking and fanning himself with his handkerchief.*

Ric. (saluting). My best respects to you, señoritas.

(*Young ladies acknowledge salute with a slight bow*)

Ros. Your humble servant, cabellero.

S. Ant. I choke! I choke!

Con. (*going up to him*). But, papa, don't take it so much to heart. Treat them with the contempt they deserve.

Ric. (*solicitously*). What is the matter, Señor Blanco?

S. Ant. Don't ask me, Agudo,—don't.

Con. Those volunteers at the corner have been speaking dis respectfully of my father as we passed by.

Ric. (*angrily*). The insolent curs!

Enr. But what did they say?

Ros. They called father old filibuster, *mambi*, and other stupid things.

Ric. If I only had my life to risk this moment, I would give them a lesson; but my country's interests compel me to be prudent just now.

(Conchita *and* Rosita *take off their shawls, come down to piano, and lay them on it.* Ricardo *follows them, and leaning on the piano, earnestly converses with* Conchita *in dumb show;* Enrique *converses with* Rosita.)

S. Ant. (*out of temper, rises and walks to and fro*). This is outrageous; this is beyond endurance. 'Tis not enough for them to oppress us, to plunder us, to murder us. No, sir; they must add insult to injury, mockery to insult—

Enr. (*stopping and coaxing him.*) Calm yourself, dear father. We will enter that in the long account we have to settle with them.

Ros. Besides, papa, don't you know that the Spaniards vent their spleen in that way whenever they have intelligence of any reverse? That victory they claim in this morning's papers must have been rather a defeat.

S. Ant. (*cooling down*). God grant it is so, Rosita! God grant it is so!

Enr. And I have very good news to give you (*lowering his voice*). General Quesada has landed with a cargo of arms.

S. Ant. The Lord be praised, my son! the Lord be praised! (*Converses with* Enrique.)

Ros. How glad I am! (*Runs to Conchita.*) Did you hear the news about Quesada?

Con. Yes, Agudo has been telling me all about it.

Ros. Isn't that good?

Con. It is, indeed.

(Rosita *returns to C.*)

Enr. I promised Ricardo to go with him. I counted, of course, on your permission.

S. Ant. Go, my son, go. I wanted you to accompany us to Cascorro, but the country is first.

Ros. Why, Enrique, are you going to leave us just now?

Enr. Yes, Rosita, I am sorry I have to; but duty compels me.

(ROSITA *runs to* CONCHITA *and* RICARDO, *and converses with them.*)

S. Ant. I wish I was young, Enrique, I do; and, even old as I am, were it not for my poor motherless girls, I would have been ere this fighting to free my dear oppressed Cuba from the grasp of those Vandals.

(*Enter* CAMILA, L.)

Cam. Master, supper is on the table.

S. Ant. All right, Camila, all right.

(*Exit* CAMILA, L.)

S. Ant. By-the-by, Enrique, at what time did Pancho leave with the pack-horses?

Enr. At six o'clock; they were just ringing the Angelus.

S. Ant. Did you send all the powder?

Enr. I packed the fifty pounds so nicely with the victuals that it will be all but impossible to find it out. I did it myself. Powder is at present more precious to us than gold dust.

S. Ant. Let us have supper then. (*To Ricardo.*) Agudo, come and take a cup of chocolate with us,—do.

Ric. I thank you, Señor Blanco.

S. Ant. Come, make yourself at home.

Ric. I am very much obliged to you; but I have had my supper already.

S. Ant. Well, I am sorry. (*To young ladies.*) Come, my children.

(*Exeunt* SEÑOR ANTONIO *and* ENRIQUE, L.)

Ros. Now, Agudo, you have a long ride before you to-night; come and have some supper again.

Ric. Very sorry to have to refuse you; but I have no appetite.

Con. Go, Rosita, I will follow you.

Ros. (*gazing at them pertly*). Oh, how dull I was! I see it now!

Ric. What do you see?

Ros. That lovers needn't eat at all; they can live and thrive on sweet words and sighs.

(*Exit Rosita, running,* L.)

Ric. (*following her playfully*). Oh, you naughty little sylph. You will pay me that. (*Returning*). She is as smart as she is pretty.

Con. She is only a child—not quite fifteen; but she is the sunshine in the house—always full of mirth and fun.

Ric. Let us sit down, Conchita. (*They go up and sit on sofa*). This is the first time since my arrival that I have had the ineffable pleasure of being with you alone, and perhaps it will be the *last*.

Con. (*sadly*). You break my heart, Ricardo.

Ric. (*quickly*). Oh, forgive me, my darling, I meant the last time for—maybe a few months. (*Takes her hand.*)

Con. (*sighing*). Ah, Ricardo! promise me that you will let me hear from you as often as you can. I will be so troubled thinking of the many dangers you have to encounter.

Ric. I do promise it, my beloved Conchita But let us drive away those gloomy thoughts. Let me speak of you. Do you remember the first time I saw you.

Con. It was before my mother's death—twelve years ago. I was then scarcely ten.

Ric. I was myself only fourteen; but I will never forget the impression the first sight of you made on my youthful heart—

Con. (*tenderly*). Proceed, dear Ricardo; tell me all about yourself.

Ric. You know, dear Conchita, that shortly after that time I was sent to a college in the United States. Four years later, my college education finished, I came to Puerto Principe, but you were not, at the time, in the city.

Con. We were then spending a season in the country.

Ric. Expecting to inherit no riches, and desiring to learn a profession whereby I could reach a respectable and independent position in society, I went back to Philadelphia, where I entered a medical college. I was successful in my studies, had all the degrees conferred upon me, and finally obtained my diploma as a M.D., when I received the sad intelligence of my dear mother's death. I was so deeply affected by this crushing blow, that I resolved to drown my grief in the excitement of the combats, and, with all my sympathies for the cause of the Union and of universal freedom, I joined the Northern army.

Con. You had then forgotten me!

Ric. I confess, dear Conchita, that your image commenced to grow rather dim in my mind. But when, the war ended, I came again to my native city—when I saw you (*rising in enthusiasm*), the sprightly child of my boyish recollection, grown into the beautiful and charming maid, I was enraptured. I felt as if an angel had been sent down to lift me from this earthly abode to enjoy the unalloyed bliss of heaven. Doubts, however, came to embitter my happiness. I feared I was unworthy of your love. The terrible thought struck me that some more fortunate mortal might have gained your affections. At last I mustered courage to declare my passion to you. Do you remember, my sweet Conchita, that ball at the hall of the Philarmonic Society, four years ago to-morrow? (*Moves closer and takes her hand.*)

Con. What delightful recollections, my beloved Ricardo! But could you not read in my eyes, even before I told you so, that my heart beat in unison with yours?

Ric. I hardly dared flatter myself with the blissful thought at first. When I became aware that you reciprocated my love, I I could no longer bear the idea of departing from you again. I went to your father to ask your hand. He didn't give me a flat refusal, but advanced so many reasons to postpone a definite answer. (*Bitterly.*) Probably he thought I was too poor.

Con. (*reproachfully*). You wrong my father, dear Ricardo! No mercenary motives have ever influenced his actions. His only objection was that we were too young yet. And then, he is reluctant to part with us,—he loves us so dearly! (*Warmly.*) The best, the fondest of parents, no efforts have ever been spared by him, even to the sacrifice of his personal comforts, in order to insure our happiness.

Ric. But wouldn't he have promoted your happiness by consenting to our union—at least if it be true that you love me as passionately as I love you?

Con. (*sighing*). Ah, Ricardo! you are cruel! How could you for a moment doubt my entire devotion to you? It is for you that I have been pining away these last four years; for you I have lost all relish for society. My only pleasure has been to think of you, to dream of you, to read your loving letters over and over. No, my own Ricardo; no more happiness for me unless I can share it with you—(*in an outburst of passion*) with you, whom I love with all the power of my soul? (*Lays her head on his bosom.*)

Ric. (*rapturously embracing her, and imprinting a kiss on her forehead*). Angel of love! Can the bliss of heaven be compared with this?

Con. (*raising her head and drying her eyes*). But, alas! Ricardo, I believe in a God almighty and just,—I believe in filial duty and filial gratitude. I would willingly sacrifice my life for you; but I value my duty above my life. I will never repay my father's love with base ingratitude.

Ric. You are an angel of virtue, Conchita, Forgive my selfishness. And now you remind me—I was forgetting that I ought to be off by this time.

Con. Let us hope for the best, dear Ricardo.

Ric. If I could know at least—I must speak to your father before I leave.——

Con. I see no reason to despair. My father thinks well of you. I hear him coming. (*Moves away from* RICARDO.)

(*Enter* SEÑOR ANTONIO, L. RICARDO *rises, and goes up to meet him,* C.)

S. Ant. Humph! humph! What have you been chattering about all this time?

Ric. Señor Blanco, I have but little time to spare, and must go straight to the point. It is in your hands to make me either the happiest or the most miserable of mortals. (*Pause.*)

S. Ant. Go on, go on. I do not understand you.

Ric. Four years ago you deferred giving me a final answer. You know I adore Conchita. I am aware that I hardly deserve her; but—were she to consent, would you honor me with her hand?

(*Pause.* SEÑOR ANTONIO *falls into a thoughtful mood.* RICARDO *shows signs of anxiety, and* CONCHITA *of uneasiness.*)

S. Ant. (*calling*) Conchita!

Con. Sir!

S. Ant. Come here, my darling.

(RICARDO *crosses to* L.; CONCHITA *rises reluctantly and walks to* C. *with eyes downcast.*)

S. Ant. Do you love Ricardo Agudo?

Con. (*greatly embarrassed*). Papa, I——

S. Ant. Speak out candidly, my child,

Con. (*in an outburst of feeling*). Dearest papa, I could not be happy with anybody else. (*throws herself into his arms.*)

S. Ant. (*struggling with his feelings.*) 'Tis hard! 'tis hard! (*Disengaging himself gently*). But come, do not cry, Conchita, don't. You love each other, then, do you? Well, let it be so,—what else could I wish but my daughter's happiness? Agudo—or rather—Ricardo, my son, I had a great regard for your father and mother. I know you well, and I think you deserve my Conchita. You have my assent.

Ric. (*grasping his hand in a transport of joy, and kissing it fervently.*) Oh, thanks! thanks! Señor Blanco! I solemnly promise you to be always a dutiful and devoted son.

S. Ant. But I suppose there is no hurry for the nuptials ; we are all going to quit the city, you know.

Ric. You have made me so happy, Señor Blanco, that I feel I can trust my fate in your hands. Fix the time yourself.

S. Ant. Well, let me see, let me see. Suppose we say, with the will of God, in a year from now—that is, next Christmas.

Ric. That will do. (*grasping his hand warmly.*) My gratitude will be eternal.

Con. (*embracing him in a transport of gratitude*). Oh, my dear father!

S. Ant. (*suppressing his emotion*). God bless you, my children! God bless you!

(*Enter* ROSITA, L. RICARDO *crosses to* R. *and converses with* CONCHITA.)

Ros. What is the matter, papa? You look affected, and I see Conchita has been crying. What has happened?

S. Ant. **Nothing, Rosita, nothing; all is over now.** Keep up your cheerfulness. I wish you would never grow any older. (*pointing to* RICARDO). There is your future brother.

Ros. (*humorously*). My brother! Why, papa, I thought you had been married but once.

S. Ant. (*suppressing a smile.*) You know what I mean. I mean your brother-in-law. (*Goes up, takes a newspaper from table, C.; comes down to a rocking-chair, sits down, puts on his glasses, and makes unsuccesful attempts at reading.*)

Ros. Is he? (*to* RICARDO.) How do you do, my dear brother? How glad I am! Poor Enrique! he will have some rest now. I have so often teased and vexed him that I found no longer any fun in the sport. ,Prepare yourself, then, to be annoyed to death.

Ric. Mind, I am *only* your *future* brother as yet.

Ros. No matter whether you are future, present, or past. I can conjugate in every tense, mood, number and person.

Ric. Can you? You had better, then, go to a grammar school.

Ros. That is a hint that I am childish.

Con. That will do, Rosita!

Ric. Let her alone with me, Conchita. She has found her match

Ros. (*quickly.*) I hope not. I am too young yet for a match.

Enter ENRIQUE, L , *in traveling dress.*

Enr. I am ready, Ricardo. My horse is at the carriage-gate. (ROSITA *runs to* ENRIQUE, L.; *and engages in lively conversation with him.*)

Ric. Dear Conchita, we must part now. (*Takes a ring from his vest pocket, and hands it to her.*) Keep this with the other tokens of my love.

Con. (*takes ring, kisses and puts it on her finger.*) I value them more than all the treasures of the world. But I must, too, give you some memento.

Ric. Nothing will I prize so highly as that white handkerchief, moist yet with your precious tears. Here I will give you mine in exchange. (*They exchange handkerchiefs. Ricardo places hers in his bosom inside the vest.*) I will carry it always on my heart.

Con. (*sighing*). Ah, Ricardo! you carry my own heart with you.

Ric. (*embracing her*). Farewell, my beloved Conchita!

(CONCHITA *struggles to conceal her grief.*)

Ric. (*extending his hand to him*). Dear Enrique, a new tie binds us closer together.

Enr. (*grasping his hand and embracing him*). I heartily welcome you as a brother.

Con. (*moved*) I trust you will take good care of each other.

Ric. That will be a pleasant duty for me.

Ros. (*Taking two cockades from her pocket and handing one to each*). Here, brothers, this is some of my patriotic handiwork. You will appreciate it as something better than a mere keep-sake.

Ric. (*looking at it pleased*). The beautiful badge of our glorious revolution !

(*Enr. gazing at it*). The Cuban cockade ! A silver star, in a red triangle, on a white and blue circlet !

(*They deposit the badges in their pockets.*)

Ric. Thank you, Rosita. The time is not far distant when that bright star of liberty shall shed its life-giving light over the whole breadth and length of our beloved Cuba !

Ros. God grant us to see that glorious day—and I am speaking now in earnest,—if not as poetically as my dear future brother.

Ric. I have to tear myself from your company. Good-bye. Rosita. (*Takes her hand.*)

Ros. Good-bye, Ricardo; take care of yourself.

(Señor Antonio *rises and walks to* C. Rosita *crosses to* R.)

Enr. Give us your blessing, father.

(Ricardo *and* Enrique *each take one of* Señor Antonio's *hands, and incline their heads.*

S. Ant. (*solemnly*). May Almighty God pour His blessings upon you, my dear children, and upon the just and good cause you are going to struggle for; and I fervently,—I do most fervently beseech Him to protect you, to shield you from all the dangers you have to go through.

Ric. and Enr. Amen, dear father. (*They kiss his hands.*)

S. Ant. Stand by each other, my children. Act like men whilst you have a breath of life left, and die, if death must come, like good Christians. That is my advice to you.

Ric. I will endeavor to follow it. Good-bye, father.

S. Ant. (*embracing him*). Good-bye!

(Enrique *embraces* Señor Antonio ; *then he affectionately embraces* Conchita *and* Rosita, *kissing them on the forehead.*)

Enr. Good-bye, my father!

S. Ant. Farewell, my son!

Enr. Farewell, Conchita ! Good-bye, Rosita !

Con. and Ros. Farewell, Enrique !

Ric. (*taking up his hat*). Enrique, I have to go home, change my clothes, and get my horse saddled. Don't forget your pass. We may meet some patrols before we leave the city.

Enr. I have it with me.

Ric. (embracing CONCHITA). Farewell again, my beloved Conchita!

Con. Farewell, my dear Ricardo!

Exeunt RICARDO *and* ENRIQUE, R.

(CONCHITA *hurries to window.*)

Ric. (without railing). Oh, what a painful effort it costs me to part with you, my darling!

Con. Ah, my Ricardo! My heart is too full for words.

(*They kiss each other through railing.*)

(RICARDO *disappears.* ROSITA *runs to window and looks off.*)

S. Ant. It is after ten, my children, and we have to rise before daybreak. You had better retire.

Ros. I doubt if we can, papa. I see somebody coming up the street who will most probably call here.

S. Ant. Who is it, Rosita?

Ros. Colonel Almanegra. (*Comes down,* C.)

S. Ant. (annoyed). What may bring him now! This is a very unseasonable hour to pay visits.

Ros. I wish you had never invited him to our house and feasted him, papa.

S. Ant. I could not help it, Rosita. He was recommended to me by one of my best friends in Havana—you know he was.

(CONCHITA *walks languidly to a rocking-chair and sits down gloomily.*)

Ros. He is a great bore.

S. Ant. I am in no humor to enjoy his company. The very sight of a Spanish uniform throws me out of temper now. Conchita, try to get rid of him as soon and as politely as you can.

Exit SEÑOR ANTONIO, L.

Con. I would rather be spared his presence.

Ros. (sitting down near him). Let us have some fun at his expense, Conchita.

Con. I wish I was in your frame of mind, Rosita.

(*A light knock at the door,* R.)

Ros. Walk in!

Enters COL. ALMANEGRA, R., *takes off his cap, makes a bow, and lays cap on table,* C.

C. Al. Good evening, Señoritas.

Con. and Ros. Good evening, sir.

Con. (coldly). Please take a seat, sir.

C. Al. (sitting down). I beg your pardon, señoritas, for this inopportune call, but I would not quit the city without taking leave of you.

Ros. Are you going to leave us, Señor Almanegra? (*Ironically*). How very, very sorry I am !

C. Al. Yes, Señorita, I must set out with my regiment within two hours. Those confounded insurgents are getting rather bold, but we will make them rue it.

Ros. What ! More troops against them ? I thought they were only a handful of bandits, who had been crushed out of existence —*according* to your last despatches.

C. Al. Hum ! Señorita Rosita, these are very grave matters— far beyond a young mind's comprehension.

Ros. (*sarcastically*). Indeed ! They are beyond *any but* a Spaniard's comprehension.

(Conchita *touches* Rosita's *elbow with a gesture of mild rebuke.*)

C. Al. (*disconcerted*). Ahem !

(*Pause.*)

C. Al. (*to* Conchita). What appears to be the matter with charming Conchita ? You are low-spirited.

Con. Oh! nothing—I feel—slightly indisposed.

Ros. Who should not feel indisposed and low-spirited, Señor Almanegra, hearing you are going to leave us?

Con. (*quickly*). Rosita! Have some sense!

C. Al. (*sharply*). You are sarcastical, Señorita Rosita. Were you not a mere child, I would consider myself insulted.

Enter Camila, L.

Cam. Niña Rosita, Master Antonio wants you for a few minutes.

Con. (*to Rosita*). Be back soon!

Ros. I will. (*Glances scornfully at* Col. Almanegra.)

Exeunt Rosita *and* Camila, L.

C. Al. Señorita Blanco, I was anxious to speak to you alone. You returned my little note unopened.

Con. I did, sir. I did not consider it decorous to receive privately a letter from a gentleman with whom I have been acquainted but a short time.

C. Al. Señorita Conchita, are you unconscious of the passion you have enkindled in my breast?

(Conchita *springs up and comes down* C. Col. Almanegra *follows her.*)

Con. (*firmly*). Excuse me, sir; but I cannot—I will not listen to you unless you drop the subject.

C. Al. Ah! Señorita! Are you entirely void of feeling? I am a colonel in the Spanish regular army, and my prospects are brilliant for a higher rank and martial glory. I will lay it all at your feet.

Con. I thank you for your offer, but I cannot accept it.

S. Al. But will you not let me at least entertain some hope? I can wait.

Con. (*with dignity*). My decision is final, sir!

S. Al. (*sternly*). You shall repent slighting me in this manner.

Con. I would not be true to myself, were I to act differently.

S. Al. (*angrily*). You forget that I have power to do your family either much good or great injury. (CONCHITA *starts.*) Oh! I know well you are all insurgents at heart. You may soon be glad to accept my services. (*Takes his cap, and salutes haughtily.*) Good-night, Señorita.

Con. Good-night, sir.

Exit COL. ALMANEGRA, L.

Enter ROSITA *and* PERICO, L. PERICO *goes up to door* L., *shuts, bolts, and locks it; then comes down to window, and does the same.*

Ros. I am so glad he is gone!

Con. He is angry because I rejected him.

Ros. I detest him.

(*A sharp and prolonged whistle heard without,* R., *after which the night-watch cries out the hour.*)

Watch (*without*). Half-past ten, and fair weather!

Ros. Half-past ten already !

Con. We must retire, Rosita.

Ros. I would like first to see my drawing materials and some favorite books packed up in some of the trunks.

(*Loud knocks at the door,* R.   *All start.*)

Con. What is that, Perico ?

Per. Don't know, Niña; somebody is knocking.

Enter SEÑOR ANTONIO, L.

S. Ant. (*impatiently*). Who is there, Perico? Open the door.

(PERICO *unlocks and opens the door*).

Enter DON JUAN *in a flurry.*

All. Don Juan !

S. Ant (*anxiously*). What is the matter, Don Juan?

D. Ju. (*out of breath*). Excuse me if I alarm you. I had hard work to get away unnoticed, and come before them. My company is coming to search your house and arrest you, and they arc so infuriate against you, Señor Don Antonio, that I fear they will commit some atrocities.

(Perico *shuts and locks the door.*)

S. Ant. But what have I done?

D. Ju. One of our patrols arrested some of your servants out-side the city, and they found with them a quantity of powder and some papers implicating you in the insurrection.

Con. and Ros. God help us!

Con. Dear papa! save yourself. Run to uncle Diego's—do, papa. (*Throws her arms around his neck.*)

(Rosita *hurries to piano and brings him his hat and cane.*)

S. Ant. (*resolutely*). I will never leave you behind while I live, my dear children.

(Conchita *and* Rosita *take and put on their shawls hurriedly.*)

D. Ju. Be calm. I will save you.

Con. God will reward you, Don Juan!

S. Ant. I will be ever grateful to you.

D. Ju. It is an old debt of gratitude I am trying to pay to you

S. Ant. (*surprised.*) To me!

D. Ju. Maybe you forget; but I will refresh your memory. It was a great many years ago. I was on the brink of bankruptcy and ruin, when your timely pecuniary aid saved me.

S. Ant. But you paid me back every dollar.

D. Ju. I did it at my ease. You did not require even my sig-nature; but blindly trusted my word. That act I will never forget, Señor Don Antonio. I am a volunteer—I have to be a volun-teer—but (*vehemently*) they shall have to pass over my corpse before they can harm you or any of your family.

Con. (*moved*). God bless you, Don Juan.

S. Ant. (*grasping his hand heartily*). You have a noble soul, Don Juan. If all the Spaniards in Cuba were like you, we would never have had all these troubles.

D. Ju. There is no time to lose. It is dangerous to go out in the street now. (*Pointing to door,* C.) That adjoining house is unoccupied, I think.

S. Ant. It is, it is.

D. Ju. Get me a crowbar.

S. Ant. Perico, run for a crowbar. Hurry up!

Per. Yes, master.

Exit Perico, *running,* L.

D. Ju. We will break through one of your back rooms into the yard of that house. We can easily climb over the wall that sepa-rates that yard from my own. Once in my house you are safe. Nobody suspects me. I will afterwards find means of getting you out of the city.

Enter CAMILA, L., *running and frightened. All start.*

Cam. Oh, Master Antonio! Master Antonio! the volunteers! the volunteers! They are at the carriage-gate; I saw them, I heard them. Oh, Lord!

D. Ju. (quickly). Is the gate fastened?

Cam. It is locked.

D. Ju. Follow me, then.

Exeunt omnes, L., *in great alarm and confusion,* SEÑOR AN- TONIO *endeavoring to make all go before him.*

(*Loud and repeated knocks at the door,* L.)

Voices (without, imperiously). Open the door!

(*Thumping and clanking of muskets ; murmurs.*)

Voice. Knock down the door!

(*After heavy and repeated blows the door is broken open.*)

Enter LIEUTENANT, SERGEANT, CORPORAL, *and* VOLUNTEERS, *acting in a riotous manner.*

Volunteers (shouting). Viva España!

Some Vol. Down with the insurgents!

Others. Death to rebels and traitors.

Lieut. Order, boys, order! Corporal, take some men, and com- mence your search from that bedroom (*pointing to door,* C.). Sergeant, you go through the dining-room (*pointing to door,* L.) into the yard. Be cautious; they are in the house; but try to take as many of them alive as you can.

Serg. I will, lieutenant, *if* I can.

Corp. Hang the traitors! I would give no quarter to any—ex- cepting the girls—they are pretty. Ha! ha! ha!

Several Vols. (laughing). Ha! ha! ha!

Exeunt SERGEANT *and some* VOLUNTEERS, L.; CORPORAL *and some others,* C.

Lieut. Search everything, boys. (*He and some* VOLUNTEERS *walk to piano, open every part of it, take out papers, &c.*)

1st Vol. Here is more damning evidence — a bullet-mould! (*Passes it to others.*)

2d Vol. Two revolvers! (*Hands them to others.*)

1st Vol. This is a neat case! Let me see. (*Opens it.*) Bits of silk stuff! By Jove! the insurgents' colors! Some silver stars! Confound them! (*Tosses case across the stage.*)

Lieut. (looking at some newspapers). These are some Yankee papers! Aha! degenerate race! They would even renounce our beautiful Castilian language! Down with them all! (*Flings papers away indignantly.*)

1*st Vol.* I tell you, lieutenant, this house was a hotbed of treason.

2*d Vol.* (*looking at a picture on wall*). Halloo! here is that cursed filibuster. (*In a rage tearing canvas with his bayonet.*) There! I would do the same to your old carcass if I had you here this minute.

Enter Sergeant *and* Volunteers, L., *hurriedly and agitated. All crowd around him. Great excitement to end of Act.*

Serg. (*breathless*). They have escaped!

Lieut. (*quickly*). What way?

Serg. Through a hole in the wall into the next house (*pointing back*). They are just through, for I heard some noise as we came on the spot.

Lieut. (*runs to door*, R., *and speaks to men without*). Lieutenant Perez, run with your men and break into that adjoining house. Be smart; the birds are there now. (*Returns,* C.) Sergeant, you go after them through that passage in the wall. (*Exeunt* Sergeant *and some* Volunteers, L.) We will catch them yet, boys.

Volunteers. Death to insurgents! Viva España!

END OF ACT I.

ACT II.

SCENE. I. *A craggy slope on the Cascorro Mountains; rocks interspersed with luxuriant trees and other tropical vegetation; a cliff,* L. L; *a rustic hut thatched with palmetto leaves,* M. R.; *only entrance,* R. *Time—noon.*

PERICO, CAMILA, *and* NEGROES, *the latter loungiug about. All the* NEGROES *carry the machete, and some of them pistols in their girdles.*

Per. Are you through with your work in the hut, Camila? Our master and misses will shortly be here.

Cam. I have made it as comfortable as I can. Poor niñas! so tenderly raised, and to be compelled to live in these mountains like runaway negroes! 'Tis awful, this war! All is frights and dangers, and you hear nothing but fighting, and burning, and shooting, and killing—(*putting her hands on her head*), Oh, Lord! May the blessed Virgin Mary protect us! Only three months ago we had to fly the city to escape the fury of the volunteers, and now we have to abandon the hacienda for fear of the troops coming so near; and the Lord only knows whether we are safe even here.

Per. You can be easy on that point, Camila. A few men can prevent any number from ever reaching here There is but that one (*pointing downwards,* R.) narrow and very steep path leading up to this place.

Cam. But if the Spaniards find out that we are here, can't they shoot at us with those big bursting balls?

Per. Do you mean that they may shell us? No danger of that, They should have first to clear away the thick woods surrounding and covering this mountain. I wish they would venture into the job—wouldn't we then have jolly times killing Spaniards?

Cam. You greatly relieve me, Perico. I would die with grief if anything happened to my misses, particularly to Niña Conchita —she is so good! I love her as my daughter; I nursed her ever since she was born.

(A sharp whistle without, R.)

Cam. What is that, Perico?

Per. That is a signal from our nearest guard. It means that some friendly people are approaching. We have two more posts farther down at proper distances; so we needn't fear a surprise. (*Looking off,* R.) Master is coming.

Cam. They will be awful tired. Poor niñas! (*Goes up into hut and brings down some wooden stools; then she retires into hut.* PERICO *retires up.*)

Enter SEÑOR ANTONIO, CONCHITA, ROSITA, *and some* BLACK

Boys *and* Negresses ; *the latter, carrying baskets and bundles, go up into hut.* Conchita *and* Rosita *carry parasols and some wild flowers.*

S. Ant. Thank God we are at the end of our journey. Sit down and rest yourselves, my poor children. You are weary.

(*All sit down.* Señor Antonio *takes off his hat and wipes his forehead.*)

Con. Oh, no; papa ! This exercise has done me a great deal of good. It is a change at least.

Ros. I have enjoyed hugely this climbing up. What a delicious breeze here! Oh ! see, Conchita ! (*Rising and pointing off, R.*) Look yonder through the tops of those trees. (*Enraptured.*) What splendid scenery ! Look at that broad sabana, covered with rich pasture, and dotted all over with our beautiful palm trees— their white stems, erect like marble columns, gracefully uprearing to the air their wide-spreading crowns of emerald-green leaves ! And the cattle, like variegated specks, scattered about ! And the whole landscape encompassed by that limpid, blue sky, and lit up by the noontide blaze of our tropical sun !

S. Ant. Beautiful, Rosita, sublime ! You are inspired. You have fired me up, too, and I will give you a bit of my own inspiration. (*Rises.*)

Ros. (*in a glee*). Will you! Oh, do, papa, by all means.

S. Ant. (*declaiming*). Here we are in Free Cuba ; we breathe the air of liberty. Persecuted, chased as we are, we do no longer bend our necks under the degrading yoke of the tyrants. We may have to live in these woods like wild beasts, feed on wild fruits, wear primitive garments ; but we can lift up our heads, and say to the world : " We are freemen ! " (*Sits down.*)

Ros. (*Applauding*). Bravo, papa, bravo! I was not aware that you could act so well, and yet be expressing nothing but your real sentiments. (*To* Conchita.) Now is your turn, Conchita.

Con. (*smiling sadly*). You go on, Rosita. I like to see papa in good spirits.

S. Ant. (*fondly*). Poor Conchita ! Why won't you join us? You look so sad.

Con. (*drying a tear*). Ah, papa ! I have such dark misgivings. A full month and not to hear from him ! If he were living he would not let me suffer so.

S. Ant. But, my dear child, I do not see any reason for your apprehensions. Our communications are irregular and insecure ; yet anything of importance soon transpires throughout the extent of Free Cuba. Ricardo holds a high rank in our army, and had he been killed or captured, we would have heard of it. More likely he has written, and some mishap has befallen the couriers.

(*Whistle as before.* ROSITA-*goes up and looks off*, R.)

S. Ant. (*rising*). Somebody is coming. I hope it is Enrique. (*Tenderly*). Cheer up, Conchita, do.

Con. I will try, papa.

(*Pause.*)

Ros. (*overjoyed*). 'Tis Enrique! How glad I am! We will now have all the news.

Enter ENRIQUE, R.; *embraces* ROSITA, *and then* CONCHITA.

Ros. Embrace me the first.

Con. (*affectionately*). Enrique!

Enr. Your blessing, father.

S. Ant. (*giving his hand to kiss*). God bless you, my son. I am happy to see you well and sound.

Ros. What is the news, Enrique? Tell us the news.

Enr. (*sitting down and wiping his forehead*). Let me take breath, Rosita.

Ros. (*sportively*). Well, do. I will help you. (*Fans his face with her handkerchief.*) Have you enough?

Enr. Be still. (*Opens his satchel and takes out a handful of newspapers, letters, &c.*) Conchita, my first news is for you.

Con. Ricardo——

Enr. Will soon be here. I sent him a guide to show him the way.

Con. (*transported*). Thank God!

S. Ant. I told you so, Conchita.

Enr. (*handing her a letter*). This letter is from him.

Con. (*snatching it eagerly*). Oh, thank you, Enrique, thank you! (*Tremulously tears letter open; retires up, sits on a rock, and reads letter over and over, kissing it, and showing other signs of joy.*)

Enr. (*laying some papers on a chair*). Here are some journals from the outside world.

Ros. I thank you for them; but give us your news.

Enr. I have such a full budget of it that I don't know where to commence.

S. Ant. Tell us about the fighting yesterday. (*Sits down.*)

Enr. We had only a brush with one of General Almanegra's regiments. I had two hundred men in ambuscade; but they were so short of ammunition that we could not do much. As it was, we killed and disabled about a score of the enemy with little loss on our side.

S. Ant. You spoke of General Almanegra. Has he been promoted?

Enr. As a reward for his cruelties rather than for his bravery. He gives no quarter, and has no respect either for sex or age.

S. Ant. I was never deceived in my opinion of him. He is cruel and tyrannical, even to his own men.

Enr. You heard of the death of the noble General Augusto Arango.

S. Ant. I did, and I heard all about Angel Castillo, also.

Enr. Angel Castillo died fighting like a hero. He fell on the very Spanish intrenchments, sword and revolver in hand, whilst gallantly leading his men to the assault. Even the Spaniards paid a tribute to his bravery by burying him with the honors of war. But Augusto Arango was treacherously and cowardly assassinated in Puerto Principe, (*indignantly,*) and his bleeding remains were most ignominiously treated—literally dragged through the streets by a mob of volunteers.

Ros. What fiends incarnate! (*Weeping.*) Poor Augusto! How our good friends are falling one by one!

Enr. Poor Rosita! We only begin. I hope you will not have to shed many tears before we are through.

S. Ant. Come, Rosita, don't cry. Let us change the subject, Enrique. How far has our Chamber of Representatives, now sitting at Guaimaro, advanced in its labors?

Enr. They have acted most speedily and harmoniously on all the most important matters. Our government will be thoroughly republican and democratic. Every liberty is guaranteed in the constitution just framed by them, and they have unanimously elected General Cespedes as our president.

(Rosita *goes up to* Conchita, *and then both go into hut.*)

S. Ant. I confidently expected that result. Carlos Manuel de Cespedes deserves that honor for his patriotism, his talents, and his energy.

Enr. (*handing him a pamphlet, open, and indicating with his finger*). This is our constitution. I call your attention to that article.

S. Ant. (*puts on his spectacles and reads*). "All the inhabitants of the Republic of Cuba, without distinction on account of race or color, shall be equally free. (*Rising.*) That will do. (*Calling.*) Perico!

Per. (*coming down, and taking off his hat*). Sir!

S. Ant. Call all the boys together, and the girls too. (*Converses with* Enrique,)

Per. (*going up and calling*). Roberto, Juan, Ceferino, Tomas, Ana, Marta, and so forth, come here, every one of you. Master wants you all.

(Negroes *and* Negresses *come down, forming a group,* L.)

S. Ant. Boys, would you like to be free?

(Perico *and* Negroes *whisper eagerly among themselves.*)

Per. Master Antonio, we have before talked this matter over; but as my companions cannot explain themselves as well as I can, they have, after consulting together, chosen me to speak for them.

Enr. Bravo, Perico! You have already succeeded in getting yourself elected into office. You will make an excellent politician.

Per. Brains and learning, Niño Enrique, are bound, sooner or later, to come foremost everywhere. I will ever be grateful to your condescension for my little learning.

Enr. Be careful, Perico, lest you prostitute those gifts by using them unfairly or for unworthy purposes.

S. Ant. But let us come to our business.

Per. (*respectfully but firmly*). Master Antonio, speaking with due respect, I will say that, were we to remain in bondage, we could not be blessed with better masters. We have been more fortunate on this score than the great majority of our brethren. Well fed, well clad, never overworked—few if any of us ever having felt the smart of the whip, our life has run comparatively smooth and happy. But the bare satisfaction of our physical wants is not enough. There is a higher aspiration implanted in every human heart, no matter to what race we may belong. You ask us whether we would like to be free. Ask us rather whether we would be raised from the condition of mere things —from the condition of a merchandise, to be owned and bartered, to the condition of *men,* and you will find the answer in your own heart.

Enr. Very well spoken, Perico!

S. Ant. Hear then, boys. By the sovereign will of the people of Free Cuba, as written down in this constitution, you are declared *absolutely* and *unconditionally* free.

Per. (*transported, waving his hat*). Hosanna! hallelujah! Boys, viva Cuba libre!

Negroes. (*throwing up their hats, and making other demonstrations of wild delight.*) Viva! viva!

Per. That will do now, boys, order!

Enr. Boys, I would not dampen your just exultation for the world; but it is my duty to inform you. You will only enjoy your freedom under the flag of Free Cuba, and we have yet to fight very hard for the success of that flag. You must help us in our struggle for liberty and independence.

Per. (*determinedly*). Lead on, Niño Enrique! We are eager for the fray. (NEGROES *gesticulate accordingly.*)

Enr. And let me give you a little warning. The Spaniards are trying to deceive you with promises of abolition; but even if the Madrid government were in good faith, and decreed your emancipation, the measure could never be carried out so long as the volunteers have control in Cuba,—those volunteers being the tools of a clan of heartless pro-slavery men.

Per. I am aware of that, Niño Enrique; and I have been enlightening the boys on the subject.

S. Ant. One word more, boys, I do not know how much I will be worth by the time this war is over; but, should we come out victorious, I will at least have my lands left. I will give you each a proportionate tract of land. To those willing to remain in my service, I will pay fair wages.

Per. (*warmly*). We thank you from our hearts, Master Antonio. Boys, viva our good master!

Negroes. Viva! viva! (*Demonstrations as before.*)

S. Ant. You can go now; and try to be honest men and women.

(PERICO *and* NEGROES *scatter up, forming small groups, conversing, &c.*)

Enr. I never felt so happy in my life, dear father.

S. Ant. We are making a great sacrifice, my son; but the greater the sacrifice, the deeper the inward satisfaction in doing what is right.

Enr. (*looking at some papers in his hand*). I wonder how wrong and iniquity do sometimes prevail over right and good! I come here across an infamous proclamation, just issued by General Valmaseda, which stamps the official seal upon the atrocities perpetrated by the Spaniards in Cuba. Read that, father. (*Hands him a paper, and marks it with his finger.*)

S. Ant. (*takes the paper and reads, growing indignant as he proceeds*). "Every man above the age of fifteen found outside his habitation without a justifiable motive shall be *shot*. Every house not displaying a white flag shall be reduced to ashes. All men and women found outside their dwellings shall be, willingly or by force, carried to Bayamo or Jiguani." (*In a passion, walking to and fro.*) But this is infamous! this is atrocious! this is fiendish! Houses burned down! Mere children shot! Women carried off by force! Are we in the nineteenth century? Are the Spaniards civilized?

Enr. Spanish writers have excused the cruelties of Pizarro and Cortez during the conquest of America by attributing them to the barbarism of that age. How will they now justify these barbarities in Cuba?

S. Ant. (*stopping abruptly*). Enrique, I must go immediately to the hacienda.

Enr. I do not think it prudent, father.

S. Ant. What is your last information about Almanegra's column?

Enr. They were encamped this morning two leagues off, near the village of Cascorro; but likely their scouting parties are hovering about.

S. Ant. That is precisely what prompts me to go to the hacienda. The houses will be assuredly burned down. No white flag shall ever be raised on any of my properties to save them from destruction at the hands of the tyrants,—never! But, Enrique my son, I have a treasure there I must try to save for my children's sake.

Enr. Your life, dear father, is worth more than any treasure.

S. Ant. It won't take me long. You know that black coffer. It is not very large; but it contains, besides the little gold we have left and your sister's jewels, many invaluable papers—the titles to my estates, my will, and other precious documents. I thought they were safe; but they are not safe against fire. I will secure them better. (*Turning to* NEGROES, *and calling.*) Boys, I want four of you to come with me to the hacienda.

Negroes (*coming down hurriedly.*) Me! master, me!

Per. Master, we are all ready, and willing to follow you anywhere.

S. Ant. Perico, pick four stout men to go with me. I want you to stay here.

(PERICO *selects four, who keep waiting; the rest disperse up.*)

Enr. Why don't you wait awhile, father? Ricardo will soon be here. I have an appointment with him on very important matters connected with the service. I will accompany you after I see him, or take measures for your safety.

S. Ant. Never mind, Enrique; moments are precious now. (*Calling.*) Conchita! Rosita!

Enter CONCHITA *and* ROSITA *from hut.*

Con. Sir!

S. Ant. My children, I have to go to the hacienda.

Con. Oh, papa! can't I have a full hour without trouble. You know it is dangerous.

S. Ant. Be easy, Conchita; in two hours I will be back. (*To* NEGROES.) Come, boys.

Ros. I will accompany you to the first post.

Exeunt SEÑOR ANTONIO, ROSITA, *and four* NEGROES.

(*Whistle as before.*)

Enr. That must be Ricardo.

Con. It is my fate never to enjoy complete happiness. The pleasure of meeting Ricardo after three months' absence is now embittered by apprehensions for my father's safety.

Enr. I tried to dissuade him from going just now, although I have not much apprehension. I hardly expect any of the enemy will risk coming to the hacienda—it is too close to these mountains, where they know we are in some force.

Enter RICARDO *and* ROSITA, R.   CONCHITA *rushes to meet him, and they fall into each other's arms.*

Ric. (*kissing her impassionately*). Conchita!

Con. Ricardo!

Ros. (*to* Enrique). Let them alone now.

Ric. How do you feel, my darling? You look rather thi   and a little sunburnt, but as beautiful as ever.

Con. Oh, dear Ricardo! how much I have suffered all this time I was without news from you! But this moment's happiness fu'ly compensates me for years of torture.

Ric. (*turning to* Enrique *and embracing him*). How are you, Enrique?

Enr. Very well; how do you do?

Ric. Well and hearty. Rosita, I saluted you before.

Ros. You did, Ri—I am at a loss to know how to address you. Let me see. (*Counting on her fingers.*) Plain Ricardo, Señor Agudo, Doctor Agudo, Major-General Agudo, of the Cuban army. My goodness! how much can be contained in a future brother-in-law!

Ric. Always the same, Rosita!

Ros. Certainly, always the same. I intend never to be transformed into anybody else. Oh! I see you carry a small telescope.

Ric. This is my field-glass.

Ros. Lend it to me, will you? I was missing so badly my opera-glass to look at the fine country around!

Ric. (*giving her the glass*). Be careful not to let it fall on those rocks. I could not do well without it.

Ros. (*pleased*). Thank you; I will take care of it. (*Runs behind the cliff and climbs up it.*)

(Ricardo *and* Conchita *sit down by each other and converse.*)

Enr. Take care, Rosita! You may slip down and hurt yourself.

Ros. (*on top of cliff*). No fear of that; I can climb up like a wildcat. (*Looks through glass, L.*) That won't do. I must adapt it to my sight. (*Adjusts the glass and looks again.*) Not quite yet. (*Adjusts it again and looks.*) That's it. How plain! I see Cascorro; and yonder is Guaimaro. (*Brings the glass to bear downwards, L.*) And here is the hacienda! It looks as if I could reach it with my hands. (*Keeps looking off.*)

(*Whistle as before.*)

Ric. Dear Conchita, I shall have to forego the happiness of your company. That is undoubtedly Colonel Ramsey, whom I am waiting for. I bade one of my aids-de-camp lead him here. Enrique, I will introduce you to a brave American officer in the Cuban service. He arrived by the steamer "Perit" with Generals Cisneros and Jordan. There he comes. (*Rises and advances to meet him.*)

Enter Colonel Ramsey. Conchita *retires up a little.*

Ric. (*grasping his hand warmly*). How do you do, Colonel?

Col. Ram. Very well, I thank you, General. (*Takes off his hat, wipes his forehead, and fans himself with his straw hat.*)

Ric. (*pointing to a chair*). Rest yourself. You are fatigued.

Col. Ram. Oh! not at all. I am not so tired as I am overheated. It is rather too warm to come up such a steep mountain. (*Puts on his hat.*)

Ric. I beg your pardon for giving you such exercise in the middle of the day. (*Introducing.*) Colonel Blanco—Colonel Ramsey. (*They shake hands heartily.*)

Col. Ram. How do you do, Colonel Blanco?

Enr. I feel extremely happy with your acquaintance, Colonel Ramsey.

Ric. (*calling*) Conchita! (*Introducing*) Colonel Ramsey—Señorita Blanco, my betrothed!

Col. Ram. (*taking off his hat and bowing*). I feel highly flattered with your acquaintance, Miss Blanco.

Con. (*bowing*). I am honored with yours, Colonel Ramsey.

Enr. I am very sorry that we cannot extend to you our hospitalities in this wilderness as we desire. But we can offer you some refreshment. Conchita, have something prepared for us. (*Conchita starts up.*)

Col. Ram. Don't disturb yourself on my account, miss. I had some dinner before I came up.

Con. You won't refuse some fruit at least.

Exit CONCHITA *into hut.*

Ric. Let us sit down, and to our business.

(*The three sit down.*)

Col. Ram. I delivered the arms and ammunitions I convoyed safely into the hands of your quartermaster.

Ric. I gave orders to distribute them as soon as they were received. (*To* ENRIQUE.) I left instructions to send some fixed ammunition to your command.

Enr. We cannot move unless we get it.

Ric. Our Chamber is in session at Guaimaro, and I have orders to prevent that Spanish column from disturbing them at all hazards. Have you estimated their strength?

Enr. They have four regiments of infantry, a hundred horsemen and four field-pieces. Considering that their regiments are not full, we may compute their forces at twenty-five hundred men.

Ric. How many available men have you got, Colonel Ramsey?

Col. Ram. Two hundred men. Many of them are Americans.

Ric. What is your strength, Colonel Blanco?

Enr. I have four hundred men—two hundred of them well mounted.

(*Pause.* RICARDO *muses.*)

Ric. We will attack them to-night. Including all, I will have
two thousand men. Colonel Ramsey, I will increase your force
with three hundred of my best men. I give you some of those
iron soldiers of the Eastern Department, whose mettle has been
severely tested. They are worthy to stand side by side with your
gallant American freemen.

Col. Ram. I saw some of them fight at El Canalito. With such
men I will not hesitate to rush into the fray.

Ric. (*looking at his watch and rising. All rise.*) It is half-past
twelve. As soon as we take some refreshment we will set out. I
will communicate my plans to you. We have no artillery; our
arms are very inferior to those of the Spaniards; and they are even
numerically superior; but some strategy, courage, and, above all,
the justice of our cause, will make up for these deficiencies.

Col. Ram. It is to be regretted that such a brave people cannot
command the same resources as their implacable foe.

Ric. Ah, my dear Colonel Ramsey! if we were only recognized
as belligerents by some powerful nation, so that we could have
some war-ships, we would make short work of the Spanish domi-
nation in Cuba.

Col. Ram. I am truly sorry that, deeply as the American people
sympathize with you in your heroic struggle for freedom, our government is so bound up by the law of nations, that it can do nothing
in your behalf.

Ric. My dear friend, I admire and love your country. My
heart has always glowed with enthusiasm for the great North
American Republic; but I am going to speak in general terms.
What is international law? By what convention, by what con
gress of nations were its provisions enacted that it should be bind-
ing on all? Mark the consequences. Here, shut up from the
world, is a downtrodden people forced into war. Ours is the
struggle of right against wrong; of liberty, in the broadest sense
of the word, against oppression in its most hideous form. Yet all
the governments on the face of the earth are against us. When
we send afloat an armed vessel flying our colors, she is treated
by every nation like a piratical craft, whilst the ships of our
oppressors are protected and honored. Is that strict, impartial
justice? Is that right? The heart of the American people—the
conscience of mankind—say emphatically, "No!" But then, that
is international law.

Col. Ram. I hope the day is not far distant when, my country
leading, a code of laws founded on a higher standard of justice
will be adopted by the civilized nations.

Enter, from hut, a NEGRESS *and* NEGRO BOY *carrying waiters
with glasses full of cocoanut milk, sliced pine-apples, oranges,
bananas, &c.*

Enr. Let us have some fruit, Colonel Ramsey. Help yourself.

This is some cocoanut milk. I wish I could offer you something better and in a better style. (*They take each a glass.*)

Col. Ram. I could not desire anything better just now. (*Toasting.*) The Cuban cause—may it come out triumphant.

Ric. and Enr. Thank you, Colonel. (*They drink.*)

Enr. Let us take another glass. (*They do it.*)

Col. Ram. As you please.

Enr. (*toasting*). Here is the health of our gallant guest.

Col. Ram. I thank you, Colonel Blanco. (*They drink.*)

Enr. Now have some fruit. (*They eat.*)

Col. Ram. This pine-apple is as sweet as honey,

Ric. Colonel, I fear we shall have to become vegetarians if the Spanish bullets spare us long. We have some cattle yet, but I apprehend a very protracted struggle.

Col. Ram. It is impelled by a love of universal freedom that I have devoted myself to your glorious cause, and no hardships shall discourage me.

Ric. (*warmly*). And Free Cuba will properly appreciate and requite your noble self-abnegation.

Enr. Try some bananos, Colonel.

Col. Ram. Thank you, I have had enough.

Ric. (*taking from his pocket a cigar-case, and offering them some cigars.*) Let us have a smoke now. Colonel, these are some good Yaras. The tobacco was raised on the very soil where our first blow for freedom was struck.

Col. Ram. (*taking a cigar*). This is then a patriotic cigar! I thank you, General; I can appreciate its merits, and will enjoy it with double gusto.

(ENRIQUE *strikes fire with flint and steel, lights his cigar, hands lighted cigar to* COL. RAMSEY *to light his, and then to* RICARDO. *All smoke.*)

Col. Ram. This cigar has a very sweet flavor and smokes freely.

(*Whistle as before.*)

Ric. What is this now?) (*All look off,* R.)

Enr. It is too soon for my father to be back.

Ric. (*looking off,* R.) It is Captain Mendez, one of my aids-de-camp. Something must be the matter. He comes in such a flurry! (*Goes up to meet him.*)

Enter AID-DE-CAMP, *out of breath.*

Ric. (*impatiently*). What news?

Enr. Let him take breath. (*Offering him a chair.*). Sit down

Aid. General, Almanegra's column is advancing on the road leading to Señor Blanco's hacienda. (ENRIQUE *starts;* AID-DE-CAMP *sits down.*)

Ric. (*astonished, but gratified*). Advancing this way! But that commanding officer must have lost his wits. We could wish for nothing better.

Enr. I tremble for my father's fate, Ricardo. Likely he is in the hacienda now. But hush! (*Lowering his voice*). Let us not alarm my sisters. We must call Rosita down before she sees the troops. (*Calling*). Rosita!

Ros. (*from cliff*). Well, Enrique!

Enr. Come down. I want you.

Ros. Can't you come up here? It is the same distance both ways.

Ric. (*slyly tearing the cockade off his hat*). Come, Rosita, I want you to do a little work for me.

Ros. We have no more slaves—every one has to do his own work now.

Ric. It is a patriotic work.

Ros. Is it? I will do it then. (*Comes down.*)

(ENRIQUE *converses with* COLONEL RAMSEY.)

Ros. What is it?

Ric. (*showing his cockade and hat.*) Coming up through the thickets I had the cockade you gave me torn off my hat. Will you be so kind as to sew it on again?

Ros. (*taking hat and cockade*). Certainly I will; but you must not be so *unkind* as to let it be torn off again.

Exit ROSITA *into hut.*

Ric. (*quickly*). No time to lose now. (*To* AID-DE-CAMP.) Captain, go down as fast as you can, and tell Colonel Miranda to have all the forces under arms, but to take every precaution in order to avoid a conflict before I join him. (AID DE-CAMP *bows.*)

Exit AID-DE-CAMP, R., *hurriedly.*

Ric. That column is doomed, Colonel Ramsey. Come and see. (*They climb up the cliff, and look downwards, L.*)

Col. Ram. I understand you, General; we can gain some of those hills (*pointing off*) and rake them.

Enr. The artillery is just coming through that cattle-gate.

Ric. (*to Enrique, pointing off*). Is all the space between that hill and this mountain covered with manigua?

Enr. It is.

Ric. What is the nature of the ground on this side of that stone fence?

Enr. Fifty yards on this side is the bed of a brook, dry at this time of the year. About a hundred yards farther this way the forest begins.

(*Pause.* RICARDO *is absorbed in thought.*)

Ric. I have my plan, Colonel. I will send a small force to attack them on the right; this will be only a false attack for the purpose of dividing their forces. As soon as they are stirred up, I will, with the main body of my brigade, assail and try to carry that stone fence, behind which they will assuredly intrench themselves. At the first firing you will start your men at double-quick, endeavoring to gain that hill under cover of the thickets. From that hill you can turn their left flank.

Col. Ram. That is an excellent plan! They will not be able to withstand us half an hour.

Enr. Am I going to take no part?

Ric. You will have your share. Should the enemy be able to retreat in some sort of order, they have only that road (*pointing off*) to take. As soon as they come out on the open sabana, let your horsemen loose upon them, and—

Enr. I will turn their defeat into a complete route. I will give you a good account of my work.

Ric. Let us hasten then, each to his post. Ah! I want my hat.

Enr. I would rather avoid taking leave of my sisters. They can read in my face that father is in danger. So I will go before you.

Col. Ram. I will accompany you, Colonel Blanco. I want to see that my forces are all right.

Ric. I will follow you in a few minutes.

Exeunt Enrique *and* Colonel Ramsey, R.

Ric. (*going up and calling*). Rosita! I want my hat.

Ros. (*within hut*). But your hat does not want you yet.

Enter Conchita *and* Rosita *from hut, the latter sewing cockade on hat.*

Ros. I am sewing the last stitch. I could not sooner find my sewing material. (*Gives him the hat. As* Ricardo *puts it on about a dozen distant musket-shots are heard.* Ricardo *listens anxiously.*)

Con. (*startled*). Where is that, Ricardo?

(Rosita *runs to cliff, climbs up, and looks through glass.*)

Ric. (*trying to conceal his excitement*). It is,—I don't know,—that is nothing,—I hope no collision has taken place.

Con. (*alarmed*). Oh, Ricardo! you are concealing something from me. Where is Enrique?

Ros. (*frightened*). Oh, Conchita! the troops are in the hacienda!

Con. (*throwing her arms around his neck*). My father, Ricardo! They won't spare him!

Ros. (*with a wail of anguish*). Oh, my God! They have captured my poor father! (CONCHITA *faints in* RICARDO'S *arms.*) They have him! (*Comes down weeping*). Oh, Conchita! Oh, Ricardo!

Ric. (*alarmed*). Oh, God! Conchita has swooned!

(CAMILA, PERICO, NEGROES, *and* NEGRESSES *come down alarmed.* ROSITA *sobs.*)

Cam. (*weeping*). Oh, Lord! Niña Conchita! my darling child!

Ric. (*deeply affected*). Come to life again, my beloved one. Before the sun rises once more on Free Cuba, your father shall be rescued, or I will avenge his death.

END OF ACT II.

ACT III.

Scene I.—*Room in Señor Antonio Blanco's hacienda; door, L. R., leading into piazza; a small window, U. R., six feet above floor; two windows in flat, barred with iron railing; door, L., communicating with adjoining room. Furniture plain; a square table, C., with writing material; chairs, &c. Time —before sundown.*

A Spanish Sergeant *discovered at table writing.*

General Almanegra, Captain Montero.

Gen. Al. Captain, have you the necessary pickets posted in such positions as to guard us against a surprise?

Capt. Mon. I have taken every possible precaution, General; but we cannot effectively prevent a surprise here.

Gen. Al. Issue a general order directing regimental commanders to be in readiness to move to-morrow before daybreak.

(Capt. Montero *goes up to* Sergeant *and speaks to him in dumb show.* Gen. Almanegra *paces the stage arrogantly.*)

Capt. Mon. (coming down). Are we going to attack the insurgents on that mountain?

Gen. Al. No; we are going to countermarch on Cascorro.

Capt. Mon. I beg your pardon, General; I do not understand our movements.

Gen. Al. Captain Montero, I had always confidence in you, and I will trust you with a secret. Clear the room first.

Capt. Mon. Sergeant you may retire until I call you.

Sergeant *rises, takes up his hat, makes military salute, and Exit,* R.

Gen. Al. My object in coming to this hacienda was not so much to fight the accursed insurgents as to revenge a personal grievance!

Capt. Mon. And have you succeeded, General?

Gen. Al. Not quite yet, but I will very soon. You know that old man whom our forces captured to day?

Capt. Mon. Señor Blanco, owner of this hacienda and many other properties?

Gen. Al. The same. He has a beautiful and accomplished daughter. I fell desperately in love with her; I declared my passion, and offered her my hand, Would you believe it, Captain? She peremptorily rejected my offer!

Capt. Mon. She did!

Gen. Al. Yes, Captain! (*Indignantly.*) She spurned me, then a colonel, now a brigadier general in the Spanish regular army! Nobody has ever offered the shadow of an insult to an Almanegra without having paid very dearly for it.

Capt. Mon. And you intend to wreak your vengeance by having her father shot?

Gen. Al. Under other circumstances her father would have been executed ere this; but I have spared him in order to bring her into my power.

Capt. Mon. How will you accomplish your purpose, General?

Gen. Al. I wrote her a note by one of the negroes captured with her father. I told her that if before the sun sets she is not here in the hacienda, her father shall be executed.

Capt. Mon. Will that bring her down?

Gen. Al. I am certain it will. (*Sarcastically.*) She is so fondly attached to her parent.

Capt. Mon. And once she is in your power?

Gen. Al. I will have my sweet revenge. I will humble her. She disdained to be my lady—I will compel her to be something less honorable.

Enter Sergeant. R.

Serg. (*taking off his hat and making military salute.*) I beg your pardon, Captain. (*Hands him a paper.*)

Exit Sergeant. R.

Gen. Al. What is it, captain?

Capt. Mon. (*looking over it.*) It is Colonel Gomez's official report of yesterday's engagement.

Gen. Al. Read it.

Capt. Mon. (*reading*). "As I was marching with my regiment on the road to Cascorro, covering the rear of your column, we were attacked by several hundred insurgents, who, under cover of the thickets, kept up a lively fire for about fifteen minutes. My troops behaved as gallantly as is customary with Spanish soldiers. We have to lament the death of Captain Linarez and Lieutenant Tellez. We had besides, twelve men killed, fifteen wounded, and eight missing. We could not ascertain the losses of the enemy." Shall I have this report transcribed for headquarters?

Gen. Al. (*vexed.*) Nonsense! Will these officers never learn to do what is right? Destroy that communication.

Capt. Mon. (*tearing paper.*) How shall I report this affair?

Gen. Al. Say that several companies of one of my regiments attacked a thousand insurgents strongly intrenched in the woods; that we put them to flight; that the enemy left about a hundred dead and wounded on the field, and that we had only one man killed and several slightly wounded.

Capt. Mon. And how shall I account for the missing men in our monthly report?

Gen. Al. Ascribe their loss to yellow fever.

Capt. Mon. Excuse me, General, but I can't see the use of thus concealing the real facts.

Gen. Al. You can't see the use! Do you not understand that such accounts as that of Colonel Gomez will encourage the disaffected Cubans who are not yet in the rebel ranks?

Capt. Mon. I speak with due respect, General; but, in my humble opinion, your course will have the effect of bringing our despatches into discredit.

Gen. Al. Never mind that. The first impression produced by them has always a powerful influence. Besides, Captain, (*lowering his voice*) those reports of continued success are a wonderful aid to our personal advancement. I will see that you, as my adjutant general, share in my promotions.

Capt. Mon. Many thanks, General.

Gen. Al. By the way, I want you to impress on every commanding officer the necessity of carrying out to the letter the instructions contained in General Valmaseda's last proclamation.

Capt. Mon. I will, General, although my heart rebels against some points in that proclamation, I am willing to wage war to the knife against the insurgents, but not against their women and children.

Gen. Al. (*growing out of temper.*) Away with that mawkish sentimentalism, Captain! War is war, and a soldier should be a soldier.

Capt. Mon. But, General, cruelty will exasperate the enemy, and render unsuccessful all our efforts to subdue them.

Gen. Al. So much the worse for them. We will annihilate them!

Capt. Mon. What will the civilized world say about us?

Gen. Al. (*angrily.*) Let the civilized world go to the devil!

Capt. Mon. We may even provoke some powerful nation to interfere,

Gen. Al. (*in a passion.*) They will never dare, Captain Montero. The very name of Spain makes them tremble.

Capt. Mon. (*meekly.*) I beg your pardon, General. I did not mean to irritate you. I was only expressing my humble opinion.

Gen. Al. Keep your opinion to yourself; do you understand, Captain Montero? Your duty is to obey your superiors' orders without any comments.

Capt. Mon. But, General, I—

Gen. Al. (*indignantly.*) Not one word more! I can dispense with your presence.

(CAPT. MONTERO *bows and takes a few steps towards door,* R.; *then turns.*)

Capt Mon. Excuse me, General, but—
Gen. Al. (*yelling at him*). Captain Montero!

Exit Captain Montero, R.

Gen. Al. (*walking too and fro angrily*). By all the saints in heaven!

Enter Sergeant, R., *hat in hand, and stands respectfully near door, making military salute.*

Gen. Al. What is the matter?
Serg. Miss Blanco and her servant are outside, General.
Gen. Al. Let her walk in.

Exit Sergeant, R., *saluting.*

Enter Conchita *and* Camila, R. *The former appears distressed, but calm, the latter greatly troubled.*

Gen. Al. I want to see you alone, Señorita Blanco. Your servant may retire into that room. (*Points to door,* L.)
Cam. (*uneasily*), I won't leave you, Niña Conchita!
Con. Go, Camila! (*whispers in her ear mysteriously.*)

Exit Camila, L., *reluctantly.*)

(Gen. Almanegra *bolts door after her.*)

Gen. Al. (*coming down,* C.) You received then my note, Señorita!
Con. (*absently*). "If you are not in the hacienda before the sun sets, your father shall be shot." (*Woefully.*) These terrible words are burning in my brain with characters of fire. Driven out of mind under the excruciating torture they inflict, I am here. Yet I know 'tis hoping against hope. (*Covers her face in a paroxysm of grief.*)

(Gen. Almanegra *stands, with folded arms, gazing at her.*)

Con. (*raising her head in great anguish*). But no! This must be but a horrible dream! Such wickedness is not possible! What has my poor father done? Whom has he injured? So good-hearted! so generous! You, Señor Almanegra, know him well. You have been a recipient of his bounty. Would you thus repay his past hospitality?
Gen. Al. I have to do my duty, Señorita.
Con. But what is my father's crime?
Gen. Al. He has been harboring and abetting the insurgents. He has been found outside his habitation without a justifiable motive, and General Valmaseda's orders are positive.
Con. And do not your human instincts,—does not your very manhood revolt against such infamous orders? Would you dishonor the sword of the chieftain by turning it into the knife of

the executioner? Would you disgrace the profession of the soldier, who should only seek to overcome the armed foe in open
battle, by murdering in cold blood a defenceless old man? (*With
deep feeling*). Oh! you won't do it? You can save my father!

Gen. Al. Yes, señorita, I can save your father.

Con. (*anxiously*). Will you do it, Señor Almanegra?

Gen. Al. Under a condition.

Con. (*shuddering*). I should have expected this!

Gen. Al. Señorita Conchita, when you came in, my feelings
towards you were not of the kindest sort. I was only bent on
revenge. But your presence has completely disarmed me,—it
has revived and intensified my love for you!

(CONCHITA *turns her face, and shakes her head in despair.*)

Gen. Al. (*impassionately*). Oh, listen to me, Conchita! You
have the power to tame the wilder part of my nature. You can
make me humane,—good. Speak only the word—consent to be
my wife, and your father is safe—nay, I will be the protector of
all your family.

Con. (*agitated*). Impossible! I cannot dispose of my heart.

Gen. Al. But I don't ask you to love me at once. I will win
your affections in time. All I ask now is your hand.

Con. Both my heart and hand belong to another.

Gen. Al. (*fiercely*). To whom? What is his name?

Con. (*calmly*). Ricardo Agudo!

Gen. Al. (*raging*). Him! one of the bitterest enemies of Spain!
an insurgent chief! Oh, Señorita Blanco. You have awakened
the demon in me. What a fool I was! To be begging when I
can command! (*fiendish laugh*) Ha! ha! ha! I have you in my
power!

(*Moves towards her aggressively.* CONCHITA *falls back two or three
steps; then stands, undaunted and majestic, daring him.*)

Con. (*energetically*). Beware, Señor Almanegra!

Gen Al. (*checking himself*). Who will dare oppose me here?
(*Advances.*)

Con. (*resolutely.*) With the help of God, I will. (*Draws a
small revolver, and aims at him.*)

Gen. Al. (*shrinking*). By Jove!

Con. (*firmly*). Advance another step, and I fire.

Gen. Al. To be killed by a woman! That would be a disgrace.
You are courageous!

Con. No, Señor Almanegra! I am only a weak, timid woman.
I have no heart to kill an insect. I would not strike a blow to
save my life; but to defend my honor—the honor of my Ricardo,
I will not hesitate a moment to put an end to your infamous
existence!

Gen. Al. (furiously). Unfortunate! You have sealed your father's fate.

(*A distant bugle is heard, sounding the attack, followed by a distant rattle of musketry; then drums and bugles nearer, calling to arms. Both* CONCHITA *and* GEN. ALMANEGRA *start and listen anxiously, but betraying different emotions.*)

Enter CAPT. MONTERO, R., *hurriedly.*

Capt. Mon. (excited). General, we are attacked on the right. Fortunately one-half of the brigade were under arms.

(*The firing becomes nearer and more lively.*)

Gen. Al. (quickly). Are our horses saddled?
Capt. Mon. I will see to it.

Exit CAPT. MONTERO, R.

Gen. Al. (threateningly). Señorita Blanco, I will soon be back!

Exit GEN. ALMANEGRA, R., *locking door without.*

(CONCHITA *steps about bewildered; then comes down C, and falls on her knees, lifting up her hands in prayer.*)

Con. (with agonizing fervor). God, almighty and just, extend thy powerful hand and uphold the cause of right and justice. Deliver my unfortunate father from the clutches of the barbarous oppressors. Spare my Ricardo and my brother, I beseech Thee, Father of Mercies, and if it is thy divine Will that some one should be sacrificed, oh, Lord! take my own life and save theirs. (*Buries her face in her hands.*)

The rattle of musketry becomes furious. The artillery begins to play. Knocks at the door. L.

Cam. (without, frightened.) Niña Conchita! Niña Conchita!
Con. (starting up.) Who is it?
Cam. (without). Niña Conchita!
Con. (eagerly, rushing to door, L). Oh! it is Camila! Open the door, Camila. Can't you do it?
Cam. (without). I can't. It is fastened on that side.
Con. It is so! Oh! my head! (*unbolts the door.*)

Enter CAMILA (*They fall into each other's arms.*)

Con. (tremulously). Oh, Camila, don't leave me alone any more. I am afraid!
Cam. No, my darling child. They shall have to kill me before they can separate us again.

(*They come down,* C.)

Con. Don't you hear the terrible roar of battle!
Cam. 'Tis awful, Niña Conchita. Oh, mercy! May the Lord and the blessed Virgin Mary deliver us!
Con. How many a noble life is being sacrificed! Oh, Camila!

every shot is piercing my heart with the pangs of death. (*Keeps listening anxiously.*)

Cam. If I could only see! (*Runs up to window in flat.*) I can't from here. The outhouses are in the way. (*Comes down.*) Ah! maybe from that small window. (*Goes up to window, U. R., steps on a chair, and looks off. It begins to grow dark.*) I see the Spaniards on this side of the stone fence! How quickly they fire!

Con. Can you see our men ?

Cam. The smoke is so thick beyond the fences that I can only make out the flashes of their guns. It is getting dark, too. Oh, mercy! I see some of the Spaniards killed !

(*Firing slackens somewhat; bugles sounding the attack nearer; Cheers.*)

Con. Oh! I hear cheers for Cuba!

Cam. Oh, Lord! Yes! the Cubans are on the fences! They are fighting with the machete and the bayonet. (*Horrified*). Oh, my God! What an awful sight! (*Comes down staggering.*)

(*Firing more slack; clash of arms; tumult; voices shouting Viva Cuba libre! CONCHITA and CAMILA tremblingly hold each other by the hand. A lurid light breaks forth through door, L., and steadily increases to end of scene*).

Con. (*starting*). What light is that, Camila ?

Cam. (*rushing to door, L., and back panic-stricken*). Oh, Lord! The house is on fire!

(*They rush to door, R., and struggle to force it open*).

Cam. (*terrified*). It is locked! Mercy! mercy! (*Runs about*).

(CONCHITA, *appalled but resigned, leans against door, R. CA-MILA runs to window, U. R., and steps upon chair*).

Cam. (*yelling*). Mercy! mercy! Help us, for God's sake! We shall be burned alive! Oh, Lord! They don't hear me through the uproar! Ah! There is Niño Ricardo!

Con. (*quickly.*) Call him, Camila.

Cam. (*yelling*). Niño Ricardo! Niño Ricardo! Here! here! (*Overjoyed*). Oh, thank God! He heard me—he is coming. (*Comes down and embraces* CONCHITA). We are saved!

(*Heavy blows at the door, R. It gives way*).

Enter RICARDO, R., *excited, sword in hand; its blade besmeared with blood*).

Ric. (*thunderstruck*). Conchita! You here!

Con. I will tell you all. (*Eagerly*). Where is my father ?

Ric. I don't know yet.

Con. (*starting violently*).   Blood on your clothes!   Are you wounded, my darling ?

Ric.   T'is nothing—may be a scratch.   But let us go out quick.   The fire is gaining rapidly on us.

(*Flames burst forth through door*, L.)

Exeunt omnes, R.

(*In order to prepare for change of scene, some patriots may rush in and carry away furniture.*)

Scene II.—*A lawn in Señor Antonio Blanco's hacienda; a stone-fence, R.; a field-piece by it and the Cuban flag displayed on the latter; some trees, L.; buildings, U. L., in flames; scene illumined by the lurid light of the conflagration.*

Aid-de-Camp, Surgeon, *and a crowd of Cuban* Patriots, *white and colored. Some of the latter are discovered carrying in wounded men on stretchers.*

A Patriot.   Viva Cuba libre!

All. (*cheering*).   Viva!

Aid.   We had a glorious victory, to-day, Doctor!

Surg.   So we had, Captain.   But, before giving full vent to our exultation, let us see that every wounded man, whether friend or foe, is properly attended to.

Enter Perico, L., *horrified.*

Per.   Dreadful! dreadful!

Aid.   What is the matter, Perico?

Per. (*indignantly*).   They have murdered Master Antonio!   He is there (*pointing off*, L) weltering in his blood!

Surg.   Come boys, bring a stretcher.   We will take him up.

Exeunt Surgeon *and two men with a stretcher*, L.

Per.   Oh, the cowards! the assassins!

Aid.   I descry several other corpses on the same spot.

Per.   All defenceless old men and youths! Savages! (*Wailing.*) Poor misses!. This terrible misfortune will kill them!

Enter Surgeon *and two men carrying* Señor Antonio Blanco's *corpse on a ·stretcher, which they lay down*, C.   *A cloak covers his ghastly body. The* Surgeon, *attended by* Perico, *examines his wounds.*   Aid-de-Camp *and* Patriots *crowd behind with gestures of pity and indignation.*

Enter Ricardo, *leading* Conchita *by the hand, and* Camila, U.L.

Ric. (*noticing* SEÑOR ANTONIO'S *corpse, and striving to prevent* CONCHITA *from seeing it*). Let us go that way, dear Conchita.

Con. (*alarmed, and struggling to free herself*). I want to see! (*Discovering her father's corpse, and breaking forth into a cry of anguish.*) Ah! my father! (*Faints.*)

(CAMILA *runs to the stretcher, kneels down, takes* SEÑOR ANTONIO'S *hand, and kisses it fervently.*)

Cam. (*weeping and wailing*). Ah, Master Antonio! my good master!

Per. (*moved*). Is he dead, Doctor?

Surg. His life-blood has ebbed away. Three bullets have penetrated his body; one of them, piercing his right lung, produced an internal hemorrhage. (*Covers his body.*)

Per. (*fervently, taking his hat off*). Oh, God! Father of Mercies! receive his soul into thy infinite bosom! (*Solemnly kneeling down by the corpse.*) Master Antonio, I will avenge you!

Ric. (*affected, kissing her*). My beloved Conchita!

Con. (*regaining her senses, opening her eyes, and staring around vacantly*). Where am I? What a lurid light! I see nothing but blood, blood! (*Recognizing him, and throwing her arms around his neck.*) Ah, my dear Ricardo! (*Weeps convulsively*).

Ric. (*moved*). My darling, try to compose yourself.

Con. Take me to see his dear remains at least, Ricardo!

Ric. That will do you no good, Conchita.

Con. (*pitifully*). I implore you!

(CONCHITA, *supported by* RICARDO, *staggers to her father's corpse, kneels down, and covers his face with kisses.*)

Con. (*wailing mournfully*). Farewell, my dear father, farewell forever! No more will you kindly look upon me in this world; no more will your affectionate voice gladden my ear. Poor Rosita! Your genial gaiety is now blighted forever! (*Keeps weeping to the end.* CAMILA *does the same. All appear moved.*)

(*Tumult and cheers without,* L.)

Ric. (*coming down*). What is that?

Aid. (*looking off,* L.). General Almanegra is our prisoner, General. (*Great commotion.*)

Ric. A God almighty and just would not let the wicked go unpunished, even in this world.

Enter GEN. ALMANEGRA, L., *a man holding him by each arm, and followed by a guard of* PATRIOTS. RICARDO *advances to meet him threateningly, but restrains himself with great effort.*

Ric. (*struggling with his wrath, and pointing to corpse*). There is your cowardly work, and that is only one of your many crimes against humanity and civilization. What do you deserve?

G. Al. (defiantly, but betraying some emotion). I do not want any of your taunts. Have me shot right off. There are fifteen millions of Spaniards behind me to fill up my place. Had you fallen into my hands, I would not have spared you a minute!

(*Great indignation among the* PATRIOTS. *Some of them approach him threateningly.*)

1st. Pat. Death to the tyrants!

2d Pat. Let us hang him!

Ric. (energetically). Hold! keep off! (*Patriots desist.*) Not a single hair of his head must be touched. I will see that justice is done.

(PERICO, *machete in hand, comes down, and kneels.*)

Per. (passionately entreating). Niño Ricardo, for what you hold most sacred ; for the memory of your good mother, let me avenge my kind master. Release that man; give him a weapon, that I may meet him in fair fight—that I may have the satisfaction of hacking him to pieces, even if it costs me my life!

Ric. (firmly). No, Perico. (PERICO *rises, grievously disappointed.*) If it were a question of vengeance, I should be the first to wreak it. It is a question of justice. (*To* AID-DE CAMP.) Captain, convene a court-martial to-morrow morning to try that prisoner. Let him be punished for his revolting offences; but let it be done according to the laws of civilized warfare. Take him in charge. You will be responsible to me for his safe-keeping.

Exeunt GEN. ALMANEGRA, AID-DE-CAMP, *and* GUARD, L.

Ric. (taking the Cuban flag, and holding it up. All uncover their heads). My countrymen! here, under the folds of this—our single-starred banner—by the blood of our noble martyrs—let us solemnly resolve never to lay down our arms until we shall wipe out the last vestige of Spanish tyranny in America. Cubans, three hearty cheers for Free Cuba!

All. Hurrah! hurrah! hurrah!

THE END.

COSTUMES AND PROPERTIES.

RICARDO AGUDO.—Black moustache and goatee. Act I, light cassimere pants and vest, silk necktie, black silk hat, kid gloves; white handkerchief and ring. Acts II and III, Cuban general's uniform—light-colored linen pants, dark linen jacket, two golden stars on collar, Panama straw hat with Cuban cockade on left side; sword, revolver, field-glass, cigar-case, watch.

SEÑOR ANTONIO BLANCO.—White beard and hair. Act I, white linen pants and vest, white neckcloth, black coat, grey silk hat; spectacles. Act II, light colored linen pants, vest, and jacket, straw hat.

ENRIQUE.—Dark moustache and goatee. Act I, white linen pants, light silk vest and necktie, black coat and silk hat, kid gloves ; second dress, colored linen pants, vest, and jacket, straw hat, spurs. Act II, Cuban colonel's uniform, dark linen pants and jacket, shoulder-straps with three silver stars, Panama hat with Cuban cockade; sword, revolver, satchel with letters, papers, &c.; tinder-box, flint, and steel.

COL. ALMANEGRA.—Dark moustache, hair cropped close. Act I, Spanish colonel's uniform. Act III, brigadier's uniform.

COL. RAMSEY.—Light beard. Cuban colonel's uniform (described above).

CAPT. MONTERO. — Dark moustache ; hair close. Spanish captain's uniform.

DON JUAN.—Grey beard and hair. Volunteer's uniform—light blue linen pants and short coat, straw hat with Spanish cockade (a red circlet with a brass button in centre.)

PERICO.—Act I, colored linen pants and vest, black jacket. Acts II and III, raw linen pants, dark linen jacket, straw hat; machete and revolver.

CONCHITA.—Act I, plain but elegant walking dress, silk embroidered crape shawl, hair plainly but tastily dressed. Acts II and III, plain light-colored lawn dress, straw hat, wide brim and ribbon; handkerchief, parasol, flowers, a small revolver.

ROSITA.—Same as CONCHITA, their costumes only differing in shades of color; two Cuban cockades.

CAMILA.—Light-colored calico dress, silk bandanna handkerchief tied upon her head.

CUBAN PATRIOTS.—Some dark linen pants and jackets; others raw linen pants; straw hats, accoutrements, machete, rifles or muskets.

SPANISH REGULAR ARMY.—Light blue or dark linen pants, black cloth coat, straw hat with cockade, &c.

SPANISH VOLUNTEERS.—(See above), muskets, &c.

NEGRO SLAVES.—Raw linen pants and shirt, straw hat; machete; some pistols and some guns.

PROPERTIES NOT MENTIONED ABOVE.—A bullet mould, two revolvers, a small sewing case, a bundle of newspapers.